Everyday Encouragement for Queens

Lisa Ann Johnson, M.A.

#NOTE2SELF: Everyday Encouragement for Queens.

ISBN: 978-1-7337020-3-4

Printed in the United States of America.

Cover Design: German Creative

Back Cover Photo Credit: Felisha English, Fee's Fotos and Designs.

Editors: Derek Crites, Francine Samuel-Roling

Get Write Publishing, 2770 Main St., Suite 147, Frisco, TX 75033

ACKNOWLEDGMENTS

To all the women in leadership who pastor others; lead companies; who own and operate their own business; who serve in government, educational institutions; who counsel others; who assist their husbands in ministry; etc.

Thank you, Queen, for all you do! Thank you for giving your all. Thank you for all the afterhours you put in; thank you for sacrificing your time, your family, and your life for others. Thank you for volunteering, thank you for all the hands you've held, all the hugs you've given, this is to thank YOU for all the times no one said it; thank you for all the times you weren't acknowledged; thank you for all the behind the scenes work you've done; thank you for loving the unlovable; thank you for giving the one who really wasn't qualified a chance; thank you for your listening ear; thank you for caring; thank you for all the time you sacrificed to care for others when you could have been home with your family; thank you for spending your own money so children and families could eat or have a place to stay; thank you for what you did to help that no one knows but God.

Queen, this *THANK YOU* comes with a curtsy! Don't stop what you're doing, but please, please, do for the Lord, yourself, and your family, **FIRST!** And, please… ***Don't grow weary while doing good!***

Royal Thanks to:

JESUS - MY KING!

QUEEN REKESHA D. PITTMAN
(THE MIDWIFE)
FOR HELPING ME DISCOVER MY OIL

To the Queens who have helped me strengthen and sharpen my gift in this season; and encouraged *ME*—***you know who you are!***

Also, to:
Queen Juli Samel
Queen Heidi Freeman
Queen May E. Hall
Queen Vanessa Haywood
Queen Marschelle Butler
Queen Adrienne stewart
Queen Nicole gunnels
Queen lorri johnson
Queen Marilyn King
Queen anTia Fitzgerald
Queen shaye anderson
Queen Marce Johnson
Queen Lynynn pittman
Queen Francine Samuel-roling
Queen tia Ross
Queen paula j. irons

& IN LOVING MEMORY OF A TRUE QUEEN:

SWEET NIECE LEIGH ANN BROWN

INTRODUCTION

#Note2Self: Everyday Encouragement for Queens, is a book for any woman in need of encouragement, but it is especially for those in leadership, i.e. executives, pastors, professionals, ministers, counselor, educators, pastors' wives, and first ladies, etc., for the times they often find themselves with no one to turn to and no one to encourage them.

Women in leadership diligently minister and encourage hundreds and even thousands of people. As a woman in leadership myself, I can remember times when I had personal situations going on in my life and when I turned to others to be encouraged, the response was often one of surprise that I was having a family or personal crisis. At other times, I just didn't want to share my pain as a result of not feeling safe sharing my personal issues. People don't always understand that you, too, have problems and that you may be having a moment of fear or doubt.

Well, have no fear! The Crownselor is here! To encourage, comfort, and make you smile as you press through tough moments and will keep you strengthened when all is well!

Journal pages have been included so you may write down your very own *"Notes2Self!"* Queen, thank you, again—for ***all*** you do!

Lisa Ann Johnson, The Crownselor™

THOU SHALT ALSO BE

A CROWN OF GLORY

IN THE HAND OF THE

LORD,

AND A ROYAL DIADEM

IN THE HAND OF THY

GOD.

ISAIAH 62:3

TAKE SOME QUIET TIME FOR YOU!

You Deserve It

One Christmas holiday, I sent a note to inform my social media family that I wouldn't be posting or responding on Christmas Day. I also went an entire year without looking at my social media accounts on Sundays.

You work very hard, Queen! You help so many others! Your brain needs a break! Getting quiet will allow you to hear the encouragement that the Lord has for *YOU*. It will relax you. A little quiet time will also take a load off your mind and allow your brain to deflate a little (lol).

I dare you to do something *by* yourself and *for* yourself, and not feel guilty about it! Queen—take some time for YOU!

#BreatheIn
#BreatheOut
#Time4ABrainBreak

Then, because so many people were coming and going that they did not even have a chance to eat, he said to them, "Come with me by yourselves to a quiet place and get some rest."

Mark 6:31 (NIV)

#NOTE2SELF

FRUSTRATED? TIRED?

Hallelujah, Anyhow

Queen, there are many times in which you feel overwhelmed by all the issues you are attempting to solve at work, in your family/marriage, ministry, etc. So much is going on in your life and all at the same time—and it doesn't stop while you are leading the masses.

In those moments when you don't know what to do or where to turn; when you don't see a way out…be anxious for nothing! That means to wait on the Lord without complaining; being fearful, or anxious. It means to TRUST JESUS to work it out. He reigns in EVERY situation! No matter what you are going through—JESUS IS KING of that thing! Repeat after me: HALLELUJAH, ANYHOW!

#NowExhale
#SayItEvenLouder
#JesusReigns
#KeepPrayingPressingAndPraizing

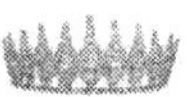

"And Moses said unto the people, Fear ye not, stand still, and see the salvation of the LORD, which he will shew to you to day: for the Egyptians whom ye have seen to day, ye shall see them again no more for ever."

Exodus 14:13

#NOTE2SELF

Let It Go!

Bye-Bye

Whenever you feel unmotivated or feel as if you are in a state of paralysis and unable to move forward—it could be that you need to let something go.

It is not easy letting go of something or someone you love, but you will find great PEACE in doing so. You will then find yourself energized and motivated to GET UP AND DO SOMETHING! You may even notice things you hadn't before. If you are holding on tight to something or someone the Lord is telling you to release…it will be okay. Go ahead, do it today. Yes, Queen—T O D A Y! Let it go!

#SeeYa
#TodayIsTheDay
#JustDoIt
#IKnowYouAreSingingFrozen

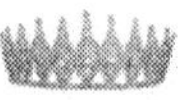

Therefore, since we are surrounded by such a great cloud of witnesses, let us throw off everything that hinders and the sin that so easily entangles. And let us run with perseverance the race marked out for us,

Hebrews 12:1

#NOTE2SELF

SH!

(Crickets Chirping). lol

Once my daughter left her opened diary sitting on the kitchen table. "Well, that's an open invitation," I thought. I picked it up and read a few pages. To my shock, my 12-year-old said she had kissed a boy! I panicked! Immediately, it was as if the Lord told me not to mention it to her. With a hand on my hip and a stomp of my foot, I rationalized, "Lord, surely, you want me to address this!" However, every time I tried, either the phone would ring or there was a knock at the door—distractions! Finally, I gave up trying to speak with her about it as it became evident the Lord was preventing me. It had been a rough (but brief) period for us. She didn't want to sing in the choir or go to church.

One day, she had to sing at a youth program. She began to sing and worship like never before. The Lord had been working on her. Had I discussed that situation at the wrong time, it may have blocked what He was doing in her life.

Not long after, the Lord presented the perfect opportunity for me to talk with her about it; a very teachable moment.

Queen, I know this is not always easy but there are times in which you don't need to say anything—just PRAY!

#PeaceBeStill
#TheLordIsWorkingItOut
#LetHIMDoIt
#PrayInsteadOfTalking

…a time to tear and a time to mend,
a time to be silent and a time to speak…
Ecclesiastes 3:7

#NOTE2SELF

#NOTE2SELF

TRY NOT TO WORRY, QUEEN!

Everything is Gonna' Be Alright

"One day at a time" is for real! I used to hate hearing that, but it is really true. Often, as a leader, there is much coming at you at one time. More times than not, it is "other people's stuff" that is draining you.

Queen, why are you trying to complete every task and assignment in a single day? Sometimes when you look at the big picture of what needs to be done today, tomorrow, next week, this month; all at the same time—it is very easy to become overwhelmed. In the moments that you do find yourself overwhelmed, do your best to accomplish what you can today and just get through today. It all doesn't have to be done in a day.
#TheSunWillComeOutTomorrow
#BetYaBottomDollar
#YouKnowWhatImGonnaSayNext
#RomeWasntBuiltInADay

Then turning to His disciples, Jesus said, "So I tell you, don't worry about everyday life-whether you have enough food to eat or clothes to wear. For life consists of far more than food and clothing. Look at the ravens. They don't need to plant or harvest or put food in barns because God feeds them. And you are far

more valuable to Him than any birds! Can all your worries add a single moment to your life? Of course not! And if worry can't do little things like that, what's the use of worrying over big things?"

Luke 12:22-26 NLT

God's word, for God's Queens.

#NOTE2SELF

#NOTE2SELF

CHRISTMAS GIFTS

Praise HIM

Don't let the hustle and bustle of Christmas stress you out. Getting the house decorated, family festivities, preparing for company; what you will buy everyone, and the list goes on.

After all, it's JESUS' birthday and all He wants for Christmas is YOU! Give Jesus your all and your praise! The best gift you could ever give. He will love it! If you do that, He's got the rest.

#GiveJesusYourAll
#HappyBirthdayJesus
#PraisetheKING

Do not be anxious about anything, but in every situation, by prayer and petition, with thanksgiving, present your requests to God. And the peace of God, which transcends all understanding, will guard your hearts and your minds in Christ Jesus.
Philippians 4:6-7

#NOTE2SELF

GOD'S GOT IT!

No Worries

Got haters? Problems? Feel alone? A daily dose of God's word will strengthen and encourage you. Read His word! It will bless you!

For example, the passage below reminds you to not worry about those who slander your name, speak bad about you, and even spread lies. Whatever your situation is…GOD'S GOT IT! Know that—you are valuable to Him and He WILL speak to you (specifically) about it. Be encouraged!

#StayInTheWord
#Listen2Him
#NotPeople
#DontBeAfraid

Do not be afraid of those who kill the body but cannot kill the soul. Rather, be afraid of the One who can destroy both soul and body in hell. Are not two sparrows sold for a penny? Yet not one of them will fall to the ground outside your Father's care. And even the very hairs of your head are all numbered. So don't be afraid; you are worth more than many sparrows.

Matthew 10:28-31

#NOTE2SELF

PRAISE THE LORD, QUEEN!

I Said, "Praise the Lord!"

A close friend once told me, "Don't let ANYONE steal your joy!" Some people have a good time trying to do that, but people didn't give it to you and people can't take your joy away. Praise on!

BLESS THE NAME OF THE LORD!
JESUS

Glory! Glory! Glory! The LORD made this day! Rejoice! Be glad, Queen! Get your work done, but make sure you do something for *YOU!*
#DoIt4You
#OneLife2Live
#EnjoyIt
#UBettaPraiseHim
#ThanksSissy

This day is holy to our Lord. Do not grieve, for the joy of the LORD is your strength.
Nehemiah 8:10b

#NOTE2SELF

Let Those GROWN Kids Go!

So They Can Grow

As I prepared to move out of state and leave my adult daughter (and grandson) behind, I will admit I had great anxiety and to be honest, I even had a little fear. It was one of the hardest things I had ever done. However, I clearly heard the Lord tell me to let them go and get out of His way because *I* was prolonging the dysfunction in her life. Yep! He said it!

Whew! Those were tough words, and it was tough to do. However, once I let her go, *oh my*!

Listen to me, Queen. I could have done that many years before, but I called myself protecting her; thus, thwarting her growth. It *is* our job to protect while we are raising our children, but once they become adults if they are not doing what they know is right or living the Lord's way—we must let the Lord do His job; and let them do their part. Place them in His hands.

#ThereWillBePeaceInTheValley4You
#AskMeHowIKnow
#Time4YouToLiveLaughLove

Trust in the Lord with all your heart and lean not on your own understanding.
Proverbs 3:5-6

#NOTE2SELF

GO AHEAD!

Give Them Their Flowers Now

We experience many transitions in life, and they aren't always easy. Be THANKFUL to the Lord for the new seasons in your life when they come. The challenges of transition can cause you to be anxious but at the same time—exciting! Through it ALL, God is STILL and will ALWAYS be GOOD!!

Be sure to thank those who encourage, love, and support you through those times; and remember to give thanks to God for them as well.
#TellSomeoneThankYou
#ItWillEncourageTHEM
#AndAddFuelToTheirFire
#ThankYouJesus

And if anyone gives even a cup of cold water to one of these little ones who is my disciple, truly I tell you, that person will certainly not lose their reward."

Matthew 10:42 (NIV)

#NOTE2SELF

Do You Hear What I Hear?

What About Us?

Queens, do you hear our children? Do you hear them saying, "WHAT ABOUT US!?"

Father, please comfort them and help them reject every lie and every seed of hate. Protect their hearts and give them discernment to recognize the inappropriate behavior of adults who spread hate and division. Help your babies stick together, pray together, and love each other. Remove fear and confusion and protect their spirits from being wounded by the hateful words and actions of thoughtless adults. Most of all, Lord, may your babies be aware and comforted by Your presence because many are afraid of all that is going on around them and in our world. Many suffer in silence because of things they have seen and heard. Please give them strength, Lord. Thanking You in advance, Jesus. In Your name, we pray.

Queens, don't forget to talk to your children and those entrusted to you; check on them and let them know God's got it *and them*—in spite of how things appear.

#DontForget2EncourageTheBabies
#TheyNeedItToo
#TheyWant2BUsedByGodAlso
#LetThemWorkTheirGifts

Be shepherds of God's flock that is under your care, watching over them—not because you must, but because you are willing, as God wants you to be; not pursuing dishonest gain, but eager to serve; not lording it over those entrusted to you, but being examples to the flock.

1 Peter 5:2-3 (NIV)

#NOTE2SELF

#NOTE2SELF

DON'T BUY THE LIES!

The Enemy is a Liar

Watch out, Queen! The enemy will try to make you think all is lost and that you are all alone. He will use tactics to frustrate you; overwhelm you, or ones to wear you out! Oh, well. Here is the TRUTH:

"Be strong and courageous. Do not be afraid or discouraged, for the LORD your God will be with you wherever you go." (Joshua 1.9)

#Glory
#KeepGoing
#YouCanDoIt
#ThankYouForYourWordFather
#JesusLovesYou
#AndHeCares

Be strong and of a good courage, fear not, nor be afraid of them: for the LORD thy God, he it is that doth go with thee; he will not fail thee, nor forsake thee.

Deuteronomy 31:6

#NOTE2SELF

PRAISE ALL THE HURT AWAY!

Thank You, Jesus

I remember watching my mother take her last breath. To my surprise, even before there were tears, "Thank You, Jesus," was the first thing I immediately said. Little did I know that it would set the tone for that period of my life. Yes, it was painful—very painful. But every time I thought I wasn't going to make it, a praise would rise up in me that soothed the pain.

Don't just praise God when things are going great. Remember to praise Him when they are not so great. Simply say, "Thank You, Jesus!" Thank Him for being there with you through the difficulty. Thank Him for His love, goodness, and faithfulness, etc.

Queen, leaders have to keep going. There are people who are waiting and depending on you. Go ahead and thank Him right now! He will love on you and help you keep going.

#KeepPraisingJesus
#NoMatterWhat
#satanThoughtHeHadU
#Holla
#Lujah

I will bless the Lord at all times;
His praise shall continually be in my mouth.
Psalm 34:1

#NOTE2SELF

#NOTE2SELF

Wait on It. Wait on It…

It Won't Be Long

Have you ever been driving and made it through a stretch of green lights? Light after light—and made them all?! Along my daily route, there is a stretch of road in which I often make each one.

One day, however, I wasn't as fortunate. I missed every green light. Light after light—RED! After missing the first two red lights, I started to get a little irritated. By the time I approached the fifth light or so, I was mad! OMG! I complained. Immediately, it was as if the Lord said, "See, that's the problem right there! Get that attitude in check!"

I thought I had been trusting Him during that time. I had been saying, "I trust You, Lord. I trust You, Lord." However, that's all it was—a thought; and He let me see my true response. Just as I had whined when I was stopped at each red light, He showed me that had been my same response every time something didn't happen as fast, or the way I thought it should. That, my Queen, is not trust.

The Lord has purpose in His timing. There are reasons why we must wait. Most often, there is something in us that needs to be altered, i.e. attitude (lol).

#WaitOnIt
#NoWhiningOrComplaining
#ThatsWhyYouAreWaiting
#TheLordKnowsWhatHeIsDoing

Wait for the LORD; Be strong and let your heart take courage;
Yes, wait for the LORD.
Psalm 27:14

#NOTE2SELF

#NOTE2SELF

RISE AND SHINE!!

Get On Up

There is much to accomplish in a day, and we often try to get it all done (in our minds) before we even get out of bed in the morning. It is also why we are often overwhelmed, tired, and stressed before we can make it out the door.

Today, try to stay focused and do everything as unto to the Lord rather than to men because it's the Lord whom you serve. (Colossians 3:23-24). Stay focused on the Father and it will alleviate that feeling of being overwhelmed.

Get through TODAY, Queen. Read God's word; sing a song; clap your hands and give Him *HIS* glory!

#JesusIsInControl
#FocusFocus
#DontWorry
#BeHappy

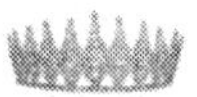

Set your mind on the things above,
not the things on the earth.
Colossians 3:2

#NOTE2SELF

UNITY

Can We All Just Get Along?

Whenever a tragedy strikes a community, it doesn't discriminate; nor does it matter whether one is male or female; Methodist or Baptist; Black, White, Democrat or Republican, etc.; because when it's all said and done, one of these days—EVERY knee SHALL bow!

Disunity cannot always be blamed on one person. How can I make a situation better? Do I speak in a way to cause further divide? Am I speaking the truth in love? Do I say nothing at all and walk away to let the Lord handle it?

Let's not wait (until it's too late) to get along.
#GodHasAWayOfBringingAboutUnity
#PeaceBeStill
#WhatTheWorldNeedsNow
#IsLoveSweetLove

Bear with each other and forgive one another if any of you has a grievance against someone. Forgive as the Lord forgave you.
And over all these virtues put on love,
which binds them all together in perfect unity.
Colossians 3:13-14 (NIV)

#NOTE2SELF

Say That Again!

Unity Begins with Me

UNITY begins with ME! As a Queen, no matter what one has to say about you; what is done to you; how one looks at you; or what others think about you. To the very best of your ability (repeat, to the very best of your ability), respond in LOVE. It may irritate you for a minute, and even hurt. But do not respond in retaliation or intentionally hurt anyone. The bottom line is, unity starts with ME and YOU. We need each other, Queen. I need you and you need me. Repeat after me and point to yourself...**u. n. I. t. y.**

Press on, Queen! Press on!

#ForgiveSomeoneToday
#LetBygonesBeBygones
#YesBeTheChange
#LiveLaughLove
#GoWatchACareBearMovie

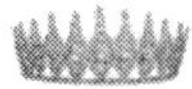

Live in harmony with one another. Do not be proud, but be willing to associate with people of low position.
Do not be conceited.
Do not repay anyone evil for evil. Be careful to do what is right in the eyes of everyone. If it is possible, as far as it depends on you, live at peace with everyone.
Romans 12:16-18 (NIV)

#NOTE2SELF

#NOTE2SELF

God's Reminder to Exhale

Breathe In-Breathe Out

Be thankful for God's reminders when He gently does so. Here is another for you. Stop and take a deep breath right now. That's it! And…exhale!

Queen, please make sure to take a few minutes daily to stop and drop what you are doing and take a break. Your brain and body need it daily. Are you taking breaks during the day? Are you working reasonable hours? Are you stressed? Overwhelmed?

Once again, Queen—The Lord's got it. *ALL* of it. He is your refuge and strength, an ever-present help in trouble. (Psalm 46:1)

#NowTurnItOverToJesus
#YesAgain
#HeIsPatient
#HeCares
#NowBreathe

He says, "BE STILL AND KNOW THAT I AM GOD; I will be exalted among the nations, I will be exalted in the earth." The Lord Almighty is with us; the God of Jacob is our fortress. Selah
Psalm 46:10-11 (NIV)

#NOTE2SELF

For the Whippersnappers

Queens Age 49 and Under (lol)

I thought I knew some things! To my surprise, I came to the understanding that things REALLY don't begin to "click" until you hit age 50! Am I right Queens? (Queens, age 50 and over).
#SayAmenSomebody
#ThoughtYouShouldKnow
#WiserStrongerBetter
#50sReallyAreFabulous
#OlderNotOld

Is not wisdom found among the aged?
Does not long life bring understanding?
Job 12:12 (NIV)

#NOTE2SELF

GET YOUR DAILY DOSE

The WORD

Queen, as a woman in leadership, I know there are often times that things grow heavy on your heart and mind. Not just the things you deal with personally, but the burdens of others as well. Not only are you leading and teaching them, but you tend to carry their day-to-day issues, also.

To help with that, before you're off and running in the morning, stop and read the Lord's word. Not only will you be encouraged but He will give you words that may come up later in the day for you to use to encourage someone else. His word will also give you instructions, and most of all—PEACE—for the day ahead.

It is amazing how we often think there isn't enough time and we rush through our time with the Lord or don't take any at all. This is how we often find ourselves "running on empty."

If you do this the first thing each morning, you will experience a miracle! A longer day! You will accomplish more of the things you desire to accomplish and go about your day with a sense of fulfillment.

#WooHoo

#HeWillRedeemYourTime

#TheWordIsAStressReliever

This book of the law shall not depart out of thy mouth; but thou shalt meditate therein day and night, that thou mayest observe to do according to all that is written therein: for then thou shalt make thy way prosperous, and then thou shalt have good success.
Joshua 1:8

#NOTE2SELF

#NOTE2SELF

GOD DOESN'T FORGET HIS PROMISES!

And He Hasn't Forgotten You

The Lord will often show you beautiful things in the sky. Take time to reflect on the beauty of creation surrounding you. Gaze at the sun, moon, and sky—to get a view of something amazing and spectacular such as fuchsia and orange sunrises and sunsets, brilliant rainbows, etc. Have you ever seen a rainbow when there was no rain? Have you seen seagulls soaring through the air when there was no beach for miles? Lol. There are beautiful happenings going on in the sky!

Look up, Queen! Hold your head high! Set your mind on things above (Colossians 3:2) and on the things your heavenly Father has promised you. Let a rainbow remind you of that!

#HePromisedToNeverLeaveYou
#OrForsakeYou
#AndToBeWithYouEverywhereYouGo
#HeMeansIt

For no matter how many promises God has made, they are "Yes" in Christ. And so through him the "Amen" is spoken by us to the glory of God.

2 Corinthians 1:20 (NIV)

#NOTE2SELF

Don't Be Scared!

Keep Stepping

Fear can be paralyzing (ask me how I know). I may get a little anxious from time to time, but I'm going to complete the tasks the Lord assigns to me. The enemy wants you to be afraid, so you won't move forward in the things of God. Do it, anyway!

Sometimes you just have to take that first step (just like a baby taking his/her first step; except babies are braver than us). When a baby first learns to walk, they keep trying until they get it. They fall but get back up with fierce determination—until they walk into the arms of that waiting, proud parent. Adults often give up after that first stumble or fall.

Queen, in this walk of life, we should be more like babies, and keep taking steps until we are in the arms of our Heavenly Father. He will catch you if you fall. He is EXCITED to see you taking those steps and ready to celebrate with you. Get up, try it again, and keep on stepping!

#ThatsRight
#WalkItOut
#KeepOnTrucking
#NoLookingBack

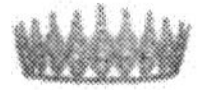

But as for you, be strong and do not give up, for your work will be rewarded."

2 Chronicles 15:7 (NIV)

#NOTE2SELF

#NOTE2SELF

YOU'RE STILL HERE!!

Yay

If you can't think of a reason to give God praise at this very moment, how about the fact that you are still here on this earth? Now, that's something to praise about!

That's right—praise Him right now, Queen! Clap your hands, sing, dance! Thank Jesus for all He's brought you through. Praise Him for placing you in a position of leadership. Praise Him for His provision. Praise Him for forgiving you whenever you ask. Praise Him for accepting you just as you are. Praise Him for blessing you over and over again. Praise Him for healing you. Praise Him for changing you. PRAISE HIM FOR WHO HE IS...Savior, Counselor, Friend, Doctor, KING! Praise Him because you are STILL here!!

This is a BLESSED day! Enjoy it! Give your worries to the Lord and repeat after me: "Thank You, Lord, for THIS day!" When praises go up, blessings come down!
#PraiseHimYall
#ThankYouJesus
#GloryGloryGlory
#Hallelujah
#WeLoveYouLord

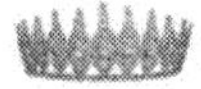

THIS is the day the Lord has made!
REJOICE and be glad in it!
Psalm 118:24

#NOTE2SELF

#NOTE2SELF

Believe It or Not

It Could Be Worse

That light affliction IS what it is...LIGHT. Yes, that problem is real, but it is not what it could be.

Queen, as you go about your day—leading and encouraging; keep your ears abreast of things others are experiencing. You may realize your problem is smaller than what it really is. Say a prayer for those having a more difficult time than you; thank God for your momentary affliction; then give that light affliction to Him. This is blessing the Lord at all times (Psalm 34:1). There is a song that often comes to my mind that encourages me not to complain. *I know, I know. I hear you, Queen*…that's "easier said than done," right?
#WorkingOnNotComplaining
#GodHasBeenGood2Us
#Thankful4HisPatience

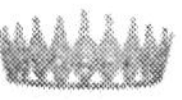

For our light and momentary troubles are achieving for us an eternal glory that far outweighs them all.
2 Corinthians 4:17 (NIV)

#NOTE2SELF

Live, Laugh, and Love

On Your Peeps

Notice how fast time seems to be going? Once it's gone, it's gone! God gives us second chances, but there are some things we don't get to do over. For instance—parenthood!

I remember a time in my life I was so busy trying to get my life together that I hadn't realized my children were growing up right in front of my eyes. I was taking college courses at night and eventually, full time; at church every other night (it seemed) to attend Bible study, choir practice, a women's group, etc. Then work, work, work!

Before I knew it, my girls were grown. To be honest, it causes me to have a moment every now and then because if there is anything in life that I regret, that would be it.

Queen, please don't miss valuable moments with your family because you are trying to get the work done. Spend *quality* time with those you love now. Work will be there tomorrow. Love on your family and let them know they are your first priority and that they are loved by YOU!

#YourFamilyLovesYOU
#YourFamilyNeedsYOU
#YourFamilyWantsYOU

And now these three remain: faith, hope and love. But the greatest of these is love.

1 Corinthians 13:13

#NOTE2SELF

#NOTE2SELF

FAVORABLE CONDITIONS?

Yeah, right. The Time is NOW!

Many times, we have an awesome idea, but we feel the time isn't right because we are waiting on our situation to get better; or what we feel is the right time, or when our finances get better, etc. Has God has given you some instructions, but you're thinking, "When things get better, I will be able to get started."

I once got an awesome revelation while watching a Christmas movie. At the end, Mary and Joseph are seen trying to find a room. (Of course, we know the story). There was "no room in the inn."

The movie portrays, Joseph going from place to place trying to find a room to stay. Mary, worn out and ready to give birth to Jesus, sat down and said, "No more, Joseph! It's time!"

That small scene was profound! I had found myself in a situation where I was waiting for things to get better before I stepped out into what I knew God was telling me to do. Joseph and Mary found themselves in a stable where Mary would give birth, with farm animals and I'm sure, unpleasant aroma in the air.

Queen, why do we overlook this part…at the time Jesus was born, Mary and Joseph were homeless! A baby doesn't wait until you are ready and in position. When it's time, it's time!

Queen, it's time to birth that "baby!" What did God tell you to do?

#ItsTime
#NoMoreWaiting
#HereItComes
#DoWhatHeToldU2Do

And she brought forth her firstborn son, and wrapped him in swaddling clothes, and laid him in a manger; because there was no room for them in the inn.

Luke 2:7

#NOTE2SELF

#NOTE2SELF

Rain's A-Coming!

And…?

Does rain or gloomy weather cause you to feel down or begin to take you into a state of depression also known as Seasonal Affective Disorder? I sure used to deal with that. Ugh!

One day as I grabbed my umbrella and headed out the door, I realized I was SINGING! I wasn't depressed because it was raining!

Queen, the Lord's light will shine on you through rain, snow, sleet, or hail—if you let It.

Thanking God for His SON who ALWAYS shines!

#TodayCanBeAGoodDay
#RainOrShine
#PraiseHimAnyhow
#GodIsGood
#ALLtheTime
#AndALLTheTime
#GodIsGood

When Jesus spoke again to the people, he said, "I am the light of the world. Whoever follows me will never walk in darkness, but will have the light of life.

John 8:12 (NIV)

#NOTE2SELF

IT'S NOT WHAT IT LOOKS LIKE

It's Not Over 'Til GOD Says It's Over! Keep It Moving!

Be encouraged, Queen! Don't go by what it looks like—even though you don't know how it's going to get done or how you will get through this situation.

I bet Moses felt a little overwhelmed as He led the people toward the Red Sea...but He had God's word. You do, too! Hang on! You're almost there! I know you get tired sometimes, but don't even think about quitting!

STAND STILL AND SEE THE SALVATION OF THE LORD! He's going to help you through it!
#QuittingIsNotAnOption
#NopeNot4You
#AMiracleIsOnTheWay
#KeepGoing
#GodIsYourHelper
#TrustHim

Then the Lord said to Moses, "Why are you crying out to me? Tell the Israelites to move on.
Exodus 14:15 (NIV)

#NOTE2SELF

LISTEN FOR THE STILL SMALL VOICE

Shhh! Listen. Can you hear Him?

In the midst of all that is going on in the world, and in my own life, I can still hear that *Still Small Voice.*

Can you hear Him? He is there. He will give you instructions, encourage you, comfort and strengthen; and block out any distractions; etc.

Even if you just read a paragraph a day, the Bible will "tell you so." The Lord WILL speak specifically and directly to you. Before you read, simply ask the Lord to speak to you, or ask Him any questions you have. (And YES, you can ask. Matthew 7:7-8, tells us to *ask, seek, and knock*).

#Thankful4TheStillSmallVoice
#ItsReallyAnAmplifier
#ThatVoiceIsALifesaver
#GodisGREATER

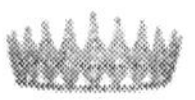

After the earthquake came a fire, but the LORD was not in the fire. And after the fire came a gentle whisper.
1 Kings 19:12 (NIV)

#NOTE2SELF

THE FUTURE *IS* BRIGHT!

And HERE THEY COME! Do you see these kids?!

They are the ones who are going to turn this thing around! YES! OUT OF THE MOUTHS OF BABES! Many of them are very young and extremely intelligent! They are extremely articulate! They are extremely FEARLESS!

Go ahead and let them SPEAK, SING, PREACH, DANCE, TEACH…whatever the gift. If you know they're ready, let them use their gifts now.

Please don't hold them back, Queen. Don't wait. Let them go. They have much to say. They have the ability to teach us right now. Help them develop their gifts but let them work now! The world WILL listen—no matter how YOUNG!

#WhenKidsSpeak
#PeopleListen
#AreYouSmarter
#ThanA5thGrader

One generation passeth away, and another generation cometh: but the earth abideth forever.
Ecclesiastes 1:4

#NOTE2SELF

SO, WHAT?

People talking about you? Putting you down? Well, let the redeemed of the Lord say, "SO!"

As in, SO WHAT! This is why it's important to know who you are; not what people say about you. Who does *GOD* say you are because people will try and tell you something different?

If you don't know, pray and ask God, "Who am I?" Get in His word and as He responds, He will give you specific scriptures. Write it down (along with the date) because the enemy will come right back and say, "Who do you think you are? Why are you doing that?"

Yes, Queen, people will try to make you feel some kind of way. Don't let the tricks of the enemy get you down. It may irritate you but don't let it for more than a few minutes. Fight back with who GOD says you are and do what *HE* tells you to do.

So, what, if you've got your own little "drum beat" going on. I do, too, and Jesus LOVES it!

Know who you are; stay focused; and (again) do what He has told you to do!

#YouDOKnowWhoYouAre
#YouAreKind
#YouAreSmart
#YouAreImportant
#AndYESYouArePowerful

"But many who are the greatest now will be least important then,
and those who seem least important now
will be the greatest then."

Mark 10:31

#NOTE2SELF

#NOTE2SELF

"EVERYTHING DONE TO ME—

Already Been Done to You"

In the movie, the Color Purple (1985), Celie said, "Everything done to me—already been done to you!"

And the Lord says that "A man reaps what he sows." (Galatians 6:7).

We must be careful to not speak unkind words about others. We must also be careful about the prayers we pray for others. Are we praying God's will or what we want for them?

There are so many nuggets in the movie, "The Color Purple." In the movie, one of the main characters, Mista,' seems to have things going pretty good for himself. We see him living it up and have it going on (so he thinks); yet, he abuses and mistreats his young wife (Celie) in so many hurtful ways (domestic, sexual, verbal, adultery, etc.).

In the end, Mista's entire situation turns (for the worst). We see him lose everything as he hits "rock bottom" while Celie is restored and reaps the blessings of perseverance. Mista' watches pitifully from afar.

Everything he took from her; everything he did to her; everything he had spoken against her—was now on him. Bottom line—Celie was right!

#PoorMista
#HeLostEverything
#WhatGoesAround
#ComesAround

And, the LORD says, "I will bless those who bless you, and curse those who curse you."
Genesis 12:3

#NOTE2SELF

#NOTE2SELF

JEALOUSY DOESN'T HAVE A HEART!

You love them so much and they love you, too—
but—they are jealous.

Queen, I hate to be the bearer of bad news, but jealousy doesn't have a heart. Just like an addict cannot control their behavior, a jealous heart cannot control itself, either. You KNOW who those people are in your life. They are very close friends, and some are even family members. Be careful what you share with such people because jealousy doesn't care about you. It is the spirit that will steal your dreams and ideas, and act like they never knew you in those moments. It will wound you with the secrets you shared with them, then strike at you like a boa constrictor! Watch out!

If you continue to put yourself in that position, then it's your own fault. Protect your heart!
#SheSaidSheWasYourFriend
#ButReallyIsAFrenemy
#ItsOkToLoveFromADistance

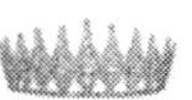

Keep thy heart with all diligence;
for out of it are the issues of life.
Proverbs 4:23

#NOTE2SELF

DON'T KEEP IT TO YOURSELF!

Give That Gift Away

The gift inside you is to be given away. Someone is waiting for it. There are specific people for you to reach, encourage, and reach that no one in the entire world can but YOU. Whatever your gift is…writing, singing, teaching, encouraging, or maybe you fry the best-tasting fried-chicken ever—whatever…someone needs it!

God has given you a gift that no one can do or say like you can. Your gift is like a wonderful Christmas present you bought for someone. Would you keep that present (gift) for yourself? Nope! You would joyfully give it away! NOW is the time to act on it. You can do it! Someone's very life may depend on it.

Queen, you are already doing it…encouraging others! But sometimes you overdo it and end up overwhelming yourself because you are doing what no one else will do, or what others want you to do, but what is that *ONE* thing God has gifted you to do to bless His people?

#SomeoneIsLooking4U
#ThereIsNoOneLikeU
#TheyCantDoItLikeU

Now to each one the manifestation of the Spirit
is given for the common good.
1 Corinthians 12:7 (NIV)

#NOTE2SELF

#NOTE2SELF

PRAY!

Harder! Harder!

Pray, Queen! The enemy works hard to discourage you and wear you down so you will give up and not pray at all. That's his job. Your job is to pray.

Remember that you are on the frontline in the battle of the Army of the Lord. If the frontline faints, gives up, or runs; who will fight for those who are unable to fight for themselves? Who will fight for those who want to give their lives to Jesus?

Also, remember that Jesus REIGNS and He is KING over every situation! Your prayers will not always be answered right away or the way you would like them to be answered, but that doesn't mean your prayers don't count. Pray, pray, pray, then pray even more.

Pay attention to those the Lord has entrusted to you. Pay attention to the things they say (and don't). Pay attention to their disposition. Has it changed? They may be in your care because the Lord wants you to pray for them. (Some people don't have anyone praying for them unless you do it). Watch, work, and PRAY!

#DontStopPraying
#EvenWhenYouDontSeeResults
#TheLordHearsYou
#HeKnowsAboutIt
#HeCares

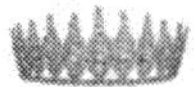

Rejoice always, pray continually, give thanks in all circumstances; for this is God's will for you in Christ Jesus.

1 Thessalonians 5:16-18 (NIV)

#NOTE2SELF

#NOTE2SELF

Suffering for Doing Good

Press Through

As a woman in leadership, there have been times in which you were treated unfairly; lied on; had your name slandered, etc. When that happens to you, it is hurtful; especially, when you have worked extremely hard to help someone overcome and rise up.

Many times, you want to defend yourself but that can often lead to a situation getting worse instead of better. Queen, you know yourself that when dealing with difficult people it is often best to just be quiet and let the Lord fight that battle.

In those times in which you must speak, say to the Lord, "Please give me the words to say; and tell me when to say them." Then watch Him set up a divine appointment for conflict resolution, and you will not believe how beautifully He will do it.

#JustStayCalm
#DontSayAnything
#EasierSaidThanDoneHuh
#ButYouCanDoIt

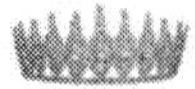

Now, who will want to harm you if you are eager to do good? But even if you suffer for doing what is right, God will reward you for it. So don't worry or be afraid of their threats. Instead, you must worship Christ as Lord of your life. And if someone asks about your hope as a believer, always be ready to explain it. But do this in a gentle and respectful way. Keep your conscience clear. Then if people speak against you, they will be ashamed when they see what a good life you live because you belong to Christ. Remember, it is better to suffer for doing good, if that is what God wants, than to suffer for doing wrong.

1 Peter 3:13-17 (NLT)

#NOTE2SELF

#NOTE2SELF

No SOCIAL MEDIA DAY

The Enemy Thinks He's Slick

Have you ever tried to disconnect from social media for a certain amount of time? I found it to be an excellent opportunity to allow my brain a break.

Queen—it works! Give it a try. Please take a break. The enemy will do whatever he can to keep you from hearing Jesus; spending time with your family and friends; having a little solitude, and he doesn't care what he uses to steal your time.

Pick a day to do this and then fill that time with something you find enjoyable that will replenish your spirit at the same time.

#satanWantsToStealYourTime
#TurnOffYourNotifications2
#ShutItDownSoYourBrainCan
#ALittleTextingIsOkThoughLol
#WhenIsTheLastTime
#YouHungOutWithTheGirls

And the peace of God, which passeth all understanding, shall keep your hearts and minds through Christ Jesus
Phillipians 4:7

#NOTE2SELF

MARTHA, MARTHA

Have a Seat

Jesus stopped at the home of Mary, Martha, and Lazarus. Martha busied herself getting everything just right.

I can imagine Jesus imparting His wisdom and love on those present, with Mary at His feet soaking it all in. He probably wanted Martha to come over and take a seat and enjoy His visit, also. Instead, she worked herself into a frenzy—cooking, cleaning, serving, hosting, etc. Her frustration grew when she saw Mary relaxed and enjoying Jesus. Of course, that didn't settle well with her and she complained to Jesus about it.

Queen, we often take on too much, then complain about it. Yes, you are doing great things and you are affecting many lives. However, sometimes we take on things we aren't supposed to and end up with no one to help us; spreading ourselves too thin; no time for self; and exhausted—mentally, physically, emotionally, and even spiritually.

In many cases, those you serve, and assist don't realize the time you are away from your family and the things you didn't do for yourself (because you invested so much time in them). And sadly, there are also those who could care less about your sacrifice.

#QueenQueen
#DidJesusTellYouToDoThat
#JesusWantsYouToLoveOnHim2

#DontBeMadAtMary

But Martha was distracted by all the preparations that had to be made. She came to him and asked, "Lord, don't you care that my sister has left me to do the work by myself? Tell her to help me!" "Martha, Martha," the Lord answered, "you are worried and upset about many things, but few things are needed—or indeed only one. Mary has chosen what is better, and it will not be taken away from her."

Luke 10:40-42 (NIV)

#NOTE2SELF

#NOTE2SELF

MANY CHANCES

But Some Things You Don't Get to Do Over

One day at the park, I saw a little girl about two years old playing. I can still hear her giggles and squeals as she ran with joy, waddling and trying to catch the ducks. She was so excited while her mother stood by on her cell phone. As her baby laughed and ran with joy, I saw how the mother was missing a very special moment. I was also reminded that many years ago, I had lost some pretty special moments with my own daughters due to my preoccupation with "my life."

Remember to be present with your family and enjoy every moment you can. Life is moving on—fast. Cherish your family's laughter, their smiles, and the joy of a moment.

Encourage, love, and pray for them, and assist the ones (who don't know) in discovering their gifts.

Queens, please hear me. Give your loved ones your undivided attention. (If you don't, the enemy will find someone else who will). Let them know they are what's most important in your life next to the Lord and your spouse (if you have one).

#CanYouHearMeNow

#Nope

#IGrewUpWhileYouWereBusy

Train up a child in the way he should go;
even when he is old he will not depart from it.
Proverbs 22:6

#NOTE2SELF

#NOTE2SELF

TODAY IS YOUR DAY!

Be Sure

Not sure you are saved? Or don't feel like you are? TODAY IS YOUR DAY!

If you have not given your life to the Lord and you want to; or you have slipped up a little and gotten off track and want to come back; or you just aren't sure that someday Heaven is your home...YOU CAN BE SURE TODAY! Make sure you write this date down because there will come a day that satan will try to tell you that you are not saved.

Want to be saved? Born again? It really is this simple...Just repeat after me and MEAN IT with ALL your heart:

Lord, I have done many things in my life that weren't right. I've done things that I am ashamed of, including things I have said and done to others, and even myself. I am a sinner, and I don't want to be any longer. I am tired of that life and trying to do things my way! Lord, please forgive me for each and every sin I have ever committed—extending back to the day I was born—be it through my words, thoughts, or actions. I mean it Jesus. I am REALLY sorry. I believe it is TRUE that You died, and God brought you back to LIFE! You did that all for ME so I could be forgiven for all my sin! The blood you shed covers it all! Thank You, Jesus! Lord, TODAY, I give up my old ways for Your ways. I want to live my life for You. I want to do right. Please live in my heart and stay. Help me do my best to live for You! Help me with the bad habits that I can't kick on my own. Show me my purpose and why I am here. Jesus, THANK YOU FOR LOVING ME AND SAVING ME! Hallelujah! In Jesus' name, amen!

TODAY IS YOUR DAY! And ALL the angels in Heaven are rejoicing because you chose JESUS (LIFE)! It's your Birthday for real! Happy Birthday! And don't be ashamed, let others know that you chose JESUS so they can celebrate with you!

If you declare with your mouth, "Jesus is Lord," and believe in your heart that God raised Him from the dead, you will be saved. For it is with your heart that you believe and are justified, and it is with your mouth that you profess your faith and are saved. As Scripture says, "Anyone who believes in Him will never be put to shame." (NIV)

Romans 10:9

#NOTE2SELF

About The Crownselor™

Lisa Ann Johnson, M.A. aka "The Crownselor™" has been a counselor, minister, confidante, and friend to women in leadership for over 10 years.

Her Bachelor's degree in Christian Counseling and aster's degree in Human Services Counseling/Executive Leadership stem from the gift of encouragement the Lord has blessed her with.

The Crownselor's goal is to ensure that women who lead and encourage others receive the same and/or healing from the word of God.

Lisa Ann Johnson resides in Frisco, TX, where she runs **The Crownselor™, Christian Counseling for Queens;** a safe haven in which women in leadership receive counseling; comfort, encouragement, and care. She is also the proud mother of two adult daughters, Akia and AnTia, and grandmother to Jeremiah. They are her greatest inspiration to ***keep going!***

The Lord is with you, Queen!
Keep pressing, praying, and praising!

THE CROWNSELOR™
CHRISTIAN COUNSELING FOR QUEENS

If you are a woman in leadership in need of a safe, confidential place to talk, The Crownselor™ will help you press through in ***YOUR*** time of need.

Counseling Services Available:

Grief
Work-Related Issues
Family/Marriage
Depression
Suicidal Ideation
Anxiety
Crisis Counseling
Spiritual Guidance
And More

The Crownselor™ is also available for:

Workshops/Meetings
Speaking
Ministering

To receive weekly words of encouragement, updates, events, and more, email:

Thecrownselor@gmail.com

Follow The Crownselor™ on Facebook,Twitter, Instagram, LinkedIn, or visit IAmLisaAnnJohnson.com.

37955662R00073

Made in the USA
Middletown, DE
04 March 2019